WASHINGTON D.C.

CRESCENT BOOKS
NEW YORK

IN THIS TEMPLE
AS IN THE HEARTS OF THE PEOPLE
FOR WHOM HE SAVED THE UNION
THE MEMORY OF ABRAHAM LINCOLN
IS ENSHRINED FOREVER

INTRODUCTION

At a private dinner attended by two of America's foremost statesmen, Thomas Jefferson and Alexander Hamilton, plans were made to build a federal capital. The year was 1790 and, as inter-state jealousies made it impossible to select any existing centre, a ten acre site on the Potomac River was ceded to the government, thereby creating the District of Columbia.

The task of raising the money to buy the land and to construct the buildings was given to George Washington and he made an inspired choice of planner for the new capital when he appointed a Frenchman, Major Pierre Charles L'Enfant. He was a veteran of the War of Independence and had served with Washington at Valley Forge, a site near Philadelphia where the army had endured terrible hardships during the winter of 1777-78.

L'Enfant, who was an accomplished engineer and architect, envisaged a city of wide, straight avenues with parks and squares and a Capitol building as the focal point. Many of his ideas were, however, scorned by Congress and he himself was ridiculed. It was only after his death that this talented man received the recognition that he truly deserved. His remains now lie in Arlington National Cemetery, which overlooks one of the most beautiful and impressive cities in the world.

Today, Washington D.C. has an area of 69 square miles on the Maryland side of the Potomac River and a large tract of land on the Virginia side. The population now numbers over two million, a large number of whom work for the government. One of the United States' most recognised symbols must surely be the Capitol, whose site, Jenkins Hill, was selected by L'Enfant as a "pedestal waiting for a monument". Congress now meets in its two houses and a lantern above the massive, cast-iron dome is lit when they are in session. A statue of Freedom, crowning the dome, can be seen for many miles.

The most impressive room in the Capitol is the Rotunda with its magnificent bronze doors portraying the story of Christopher Columbus. Around the walls hang enormous oil paintings depicting important scenes from American history. It is here that Presidents, statesmen and other important dignitaries lie in State. The nearby Statuary Hall was originally the legislative chamber of the House of Representatives and it is renowned for its statues and its strange reverberating acoustics.

Washington's other equally famous building is the White House – official residence of the President of the United States. Its elaborate construction of white-painted sandstone, in the Italian Renaissance style, was designed by James Hoban, who also restored it after it was burned by the British in 1814. In 1948, the White House was found to be in a poor state of repair and during the following four years it was completely renovated. Later, much of the décor was remodelled by Mrs John F. Kennedy to reflect various periods with as much authenticity as possible. The East Room is the most celebrated and is used for weddings, receptions and other ceremonial occasions. The Green, Red and Blue Rooms, which need no explanation as to colour schemes, all contain exquisite furniture and fine paintings.

South from the White House, across its sweeping lawns and over Constitution Avenue, is the world's tallest masonry structure – the Washington Monument. This distinctive landmark boasts 898 steps, from the top of which, on a clear day, breathtaking views stretching for up to 45 miles may be seen.

The city's other monuments include the Lincoln Memorial and the Jefferson Memorial. The former is in the style of a Greek Temple, with 36 columns representing the number of states in the Union at the time of Lincoln's death, and 56 steps, one for each year of his life. Inside is the statue of the great man whose life was ended so tragically by John Wilkes Booth, a Confederate fanatic, in a Washington theatre.

Resembling his home, Monticello, is the Jefferson Memorial which encloses a 19 foot bronze statue of the 3rd President, who was largely responsible for the drafting of the Declaration of Independence.

Amongst Washington's other classical buildings are the Supreme Court, with its vast Corinthian columns, the Library of Congress – one of the world's most comprehensive libraries – and the National Archives Building, which houses America's most precious documents, including the Declaration of Independence and the Constitution.

In contrast to these gleaming white buildings is the natural sandstone of the Smithsonian Institute, begun in 1846 and named after James Smithson, a British scientist who left a bequest of over half a million dollars to the United States to create "an establishment for the increase and diffusion of knowledge among men". Although he never visited America during his lifetime his remains are now interred in a crypt beneath the old tower. Smithson's money was used to build a great museum, an art gallery, a zoo park and an astrophysical observatory.

Across the Memorial Bridge from the Lincoln Memorial is Arlington National Cemetery which was first used for the burial of troops killed during the Civil War. More recently Arlington has attracted world-wide attention as the resting-place of President John F. Kennedy and his Senator brother, Robert.

Just a few miles down the Potomac River is Mount Vernon, the estate and home where George Washington lived and died, and where by his own wish he is buried, alongside his wife Martha.

Facing page: the massive marble statue of Abraham Lincoln in the Lincoln Memorial.

As the national capital of the United States of America, Washington D.C. is crowded with monuments and memorials honoring the great men of the past. Above: the Robert A. Taft Memorial. Taft was chosen by a Senate committee in 1957 as one of the five outstanding senators in the nation's history. The money for the memorial was raised voluntarily and used to construct the ten-foot-tall statue and the simple bell tower which backs it. The 27 bells are rung regularly. Top right: the Lincoln Memorial, completed in 1922. Center right: the Iwo Jima Memorial. Bottom right: the Memorial Amphitheater in Arlington National Cemetery which is used for Memorial and Veteran Day services. Facing page: the attractive interior of the Pavilion at the Old Post Office, an indoor mall comprising shops, restaurants and entertainments.

The Lincoln Memorial (right and top right)
stands at the western end of the
Reflecting Pool and on the eastern bank of
the Potomac. The solid majesty of the
temple-like building is a fitting prelude
to the awesome statue which stands within.
Each of the 36 columns represents a member
state of the Union at the time of
Lincoln's death, while on the walls above
the colonnade are inscribed the names of
the 48 states at the time of the
memorial's completion. Above: the dome of
the Capitol. Top center: the Washington
Monument.

These pages: the National
Air and Space Museum
houses the world's finest
collection of
aeronautical as well as
astronautical exhibits.
Because of its sheer
size, only a small part
of the collection can be
displayed at any one time
and many exhibits are
frequently loaned to
other museums throughout
the world.

Officially the Cathedral Church of Saint Peter and Saint Paul of the Episcopal Diocese of Washington, the glorious Gothic masterpiece (above and top center left) is more usually known as the Washington Cathedral. The foundation stone was laid in 1907 and the completed nave was dedicated in 1976. A legacy from James Smithson, whose tomb (top right) lies in the "Castle" (left), was the start of the Smithsonian Institution. Top center right: Explorer's Hall, National Geographic Society. Top left: George Washington by Gilbert Scott, National Portrait Gallery.

Above: a self-explanatory stone on the
Ellipse, before the White House. Top: the
Washington Monument. Left: the U.S. Grant
Memorial and the Capitol.

13

VIET VETS

MEM POST

339

The Vietman Veterans Memorial (these pages),
with its the somber, black granite walls and
statue of three Vietnam soldiers (above),
strongly evokes the memory of the brave men
who lost their lives in the call of duty.

The National Gallery of Art on The Mall contains many fine paintings including: (top left) "Oarsman at Chatou" by Auguste Renoir; (top center left) "the Lovers" by Picasso; (top center right) "Odalisque with raised arms" by Matisse; (top right) "the Honourable Mrs. Graham" by Thomas Gainsborough; (above right) "Small Cowper Madonna" by Raphael; (above left) "At the Races" by Manet; (left) "the Artist's Father" by Paul Cezanne and (far left) "Girl with a Watering Can" by Renoir.

"Time and accident are committing daily havoc" warned Thomas Jefferson with reference to government records, but nobody listened to him. It was not until the 1930s that the National Archives of the United States (bottom, far right) was established to catalogue, sift through and care for official records. Above and top: the Thomas Jefferson Memorial. Right: the Capitol. Top far right: the Lincoln Memorial.

IN THIS TEMPLE
AS IN THE HEARTS OF THE PEOPLE
FOR WHOM HE SAVED THE UNION
THE MEMORY OF ABRAHAM LINCOLN
IS ENSHRINED FOREVER

ARCHIVES OF THE UNITED STATES OF AMERICA

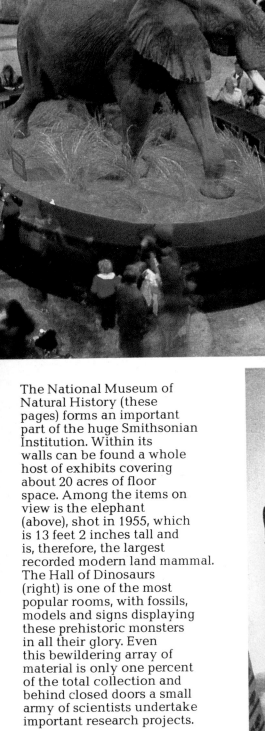

The National Museum of
Natural History (these
pages) forms an important
part of the huge Smithsonian
Institution. Within its
walls can be found a whole
host of exhibits covering
about 20 acres of floor
space. Among the items on
view is the elephant
(above), shot in 1955, which
is 13 feet 2 inches tall and
is, therefore, the largest
recorded modern land mammal.
The Hall of Dinosaurs
(right) is one of the most
popular rooms, with fossils,
models and signs displaying
these prehistoric monsters
in all their glory. Even
this bewildering array of
material is only one percent
of the total collection and
behind closed doors a small
army of scientists undertake
important research projects.

Right: the Arts and Industries Building, (bottom) the National Visitor Center, formerly Union Station and (facing page left inset) the majestic figure of Abraham Lincoln, situated inside the famous memorial designed by Henry Bacon. Remaining pictures: the Washington Monument.

The GEORGE WASHINGTON
MASONIC NATIONAL MEMORIAL

The Thomas Jefferson Memorial (main picture
right and top) was constructed on the south bank
of the Tidal Basin earlier this century. It
honors the chief architect of the Declaration of
Independence and the nation's third President.
Above: the George Washington Masonic National
Memorial. Inset top right: the Lincoln Memorial
and (inset right) the White House.

Occupying hundreds of acres on the slopes above the Potomac, Arlington National Cemetery (these pages) contains the graves of thousands of soldiers as well as that of President Kennedy (inset left). Overleaf: the Vietnam Veterans Memorial in The Mall.

IE PIPPINS Sr ·
EMP · CECIL Y WARE ·
KLIN V BRODNIK ·
W VITHEE ·
B BREWER Jr ·
SN F FRANK ·
AMES ·
MS Jr · FREDERICK E SMITH ·
AYRES ·
E B McCLOUD ·
ASEBOLT ·
ANKLIN D R GILBERT ·
JOHNSON ·
DLETON MARK L MORGAN ·
URTIS J McGEE ·
WOLCHESKI ·
BER ROBERTS ·
NARANJO Jr ·
M YOUNG · ALBERT F BAIRD ·
RAWLEY ONNIE R KING ·
DONALD BOBLISH ·
NETT G JENKINS ·
GREENE ·
RY C ALLEN ·
ENTA S S COCCHIARA
LLIAM W
R ATHERDEN ·
SEAN P DOD
DDARD · HARR
HARRY P HE
WILLIAM J H
LOPEZ Jr ·
PETER G S
OSEPH R R
ALFRE
WETZE S D
GARD MICHA
ILLIE
BEAU
W EDW
RICKEY D
THOMAS A Jr
KITTS · FREDER
TOMMY R

DAVID M DAVIES · DONALD
WILLIAM D HASTY · JAMES MC
NORMAN N MILLER · PAUL R H
THURMAN W OWEN · DANIEL
KEITH L SHIPP · JIMMY B TAYLO
RALPH M WILLIAMS · RICHARD
· GARY D NAIL · DAVID E HORNE
ARTHUR C MORRIS Jr · KENNET
DONOVAN J PRUETT · TOMMIE
JACK D GILBERT · FRANKLIN E HO
JAMES W BROWN · GERMAN
KEITH W KAUFFMAN · HAROLD
LAWRENCE McCREA · CHARLIE R
EDWARD M STANCHEK · FRANKLI
ARNOLD WOODSON · BERNARD
DENNIS P COOK · JAMES W CATE
· ROBERT A KREUZIGER · JOHN W LA
THOMAS J RALSTON · JACK A SMIT
JOHN M BROWN III · MARTIN
ARTHUR J BAYLOR · THOMAS T WA
GEORGE L SAMUELS · CHARLES M
RALPH S KOROLZYK · THOMA
RONALD T SHELTON · THOMA
HOWARD

Catering to the tastes of civil servants and visitors to the capital, the restaurants of Washington (far right) display a variety and diversity which enables them to claim that they have "something for everyone." The historic area of Georgetown includes many fine residences such as those in O Street (top right), the Marbury-Kennedy House (above) and the Old Stone House (top left), as well as the Episcopal church (right).

Top right, far right and center right: just three of the Hirshhorn Museum's many modern sculptures. The National Gallery of Art (above) has increased its space by using the East Building (right and top), designed by I.M. Pei.

Top: the graceful Thomas Jefferson Memorial reflected in the waters of the Tidal Basin. Right: elegant Arlington House, the former home of Robert E. Lee, is the centerpiece of Arlington National Cemetery. Above and facing page: the Washington Monument.

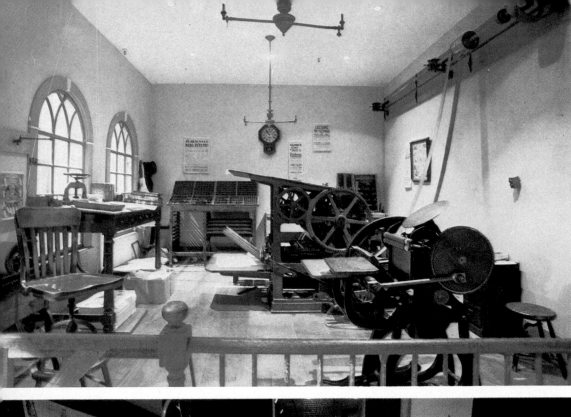

The National Museum of History and Technology has a wealth of exhibits dealing with the nation's scientific and technological development. Items in the museum include: (top left) a reconstruction of an early newspaper bureau; (above) a 1913 Harley Davidson motorcycle; (right) a Prairie Schooner wagon and (far right) an old steam locomotive. Top right: the Baldwin Locomotive in the Arts and Industries Building.

The National Gallery of Art, whose superb rotunda is shown (top right), began with a gift from a former Secretary of the Treasury, Andrew Mellon. Today, it houses one of the world's most important collections of art from the 13th century to the present day. Above: the Thomas Jefferson Memorial. Top center: the Capitol. Right: the Washington Monument. Bottom right: the Lincoln Memorial.

Tracing the relatively recent history of man's airborne achievements, the galleries of the National Air and Space Museum (these pages) house a unique collection of fascinating exhibits. The large, modern building on Independence Avenue has sheer, white walls which contain huge halls with lofty roofs ideal for the display of aircraft, many of which are suspended high overhead.

Arlington National Cemetery (these pages) contains many tombs, but few can be as famous as those of the two Kennedy brothers (right) and the unknown soldier (top left and inset far right) which is perpetually watched-over by a member of the Old Guard (above). Arlington House (inset top right) was once the home of Robert E. Lee.

UNDER AUTHORITY OF PUBLIC RESOLUTION 67, OF THE 66TH CONGRESS, APPROVED MARCH 4, 1921, AN UNKNOWN AMERICAN SOLDIER WAS EXHUMED FROM EACH OF THE FOUR AMERICAN CEMETERIES IN FRANCE. THEY WERE PLACED IN IDENTICAL CASKETS AND ASSEMBLED AT CHALONS SUR MARNE.

THE UNKNOWN SOLDIER WAS SELECTED ON OCTOBER 24, 1921. SERGEANT EDWARD F. YOUNGER, U.S. ARMY, CARRYING A SPRAY OF WHITE ROSES, ENTERED THE ROOM WHERE THE FOUR UNMARKED FLAG-DRAPED CASKETS WERE RESTING. HE SLOWLY CIRCLED, SILENTLY PLACING THE ROSES ON ONE OF THE CASKETS. THUS THE UNKNOWN SOLDIER WAS OFFICIALLY DESIGNATED. THE THREE REMAINING UNKNOWN AMERICANS WERE THEN RETURNED TO THE MEUSE ARGONNE CEMETERY.

THE UNKNOWN SOLDIER WAS PLACED ABOARD THE U.S. CRUISER OLYMPIA, WHICH ARRIVED AT THE NATION'S CAPITOL ON NOVEMBER 9, 1921. THE HONORED REMAINS WERE TAKEN TO THE ROTUNDA OF THE UNITED STATES CAPITOL, TO REST IN STATE UNTIL ARMISTICE DAY. ON NOVEMBER 11, THE UNKNOWN SOLDIER WAS MOVED TO THE MEMORIAL AMPHITHEATER, IN ARLINGTON NATIONAL CEMETERY. AFTER THE SERVICES IN THE AMPHITHEATER, THE REMAINS WERE BORNE TO THE SARCOPHAGUS FOR BRIEF COMMITTAL RITES. THE IMPRESSIVE CEREMONY CLOSED WITH THREE SALVOS OF ARTILLERY, THE SOUNDING OF TAPS AND THE NATIONAL SALUTE.

UNDER AUTHORITY OF PUBLIC LAW 429, 79TH CONGRESS, APPROVED 24 JUNE 1946, 13 UNKNOWN AMERICANS WHO LOST THEIR LIVES WHILE SERVING OVERSEAS IN THE ARMED FORCES OF THE UNITED STATES DURING WORLD WAR II WERE EXHUMED FROM AMERICAN CEMETERIES IN EUROPE AND AFRICA, AND SHIPPED IN IDENTICAL CASKETS TO EPINAL, FRANCE. MAJOR GENERAL EDWARD J. O'NEILL, U.S. ARMY, ON MAY 12, 1958, SOLEMNLY CHOSE FROM AMONG THESE CASKETS ONE TO BE DESIGNATED AS THE TRANS-ATLANTIC CANDIDATE UNKNOWN. THE REMAINING UNKNOWN AMERICANS WERE REINTERRED.

THE REMAINS OF TWO UNKNOWN AMERICANS WERE DISINTERRED ON APRIL 15, 1958 FROM THE NATIONAL CEMETERY OF THE PACIFIC, HAWAII, AND FOUR UNKNOWNS WERE DISINTERRED FROM THE FORT MCKINLEY AMERICAN CEMETERY AND MEMORIAL, IN THE PHILIPPINES. THE SIX UNKNOWNS WERE THEN TAKEN TO HICKAM AIR FORCE BASE, WHERE ON MAY 16, 1958, COLONEL GLENN T. EAGLESTON, U.S. AIR FORCE, PLACED A WHITE CARNATION LEI, SELECTING CANDIDATE-UNKNOWN TO REPRESENT THE TRANS-PACIFIC PHASE OF WORLD WAR II. THE FIVE OTHER CASKETS WERE REINTERRED.

THE CANDIDATE-UNKNOWN WAS THEN TRANSPORTED TO THE CRUISER CANBERRA WHERE THE FINAL SELECTION OF WORLD WAR II UNKNOWN TOOK PLACE.

ON THE AFTER-MISSILE DECK OF THE CANBERRA, HOSPITALMAN FIRST CLASS WILLIAM R. CHARETTE, THE NAVY'S ONLY ACTIVE ENLISTED HOLDER OF THE MEDAL OF HONOR, HAD THE DISTINCTION OF MAKING THE SELECTION OF THE WORLD WAR II UNKNOWN. AFTER A MOMENTS HESITATION HE PLACED A WREATH AT THE FOOT OF THE CASKET ON HIS RIGHT. THIS WAS THE UNKNOWN OF WORLD WAR II. THE CANDIDATE-UNKNOWN NOT SELECTED RECEIVED A SAILOR'S SOLEMN BURIAL AT SEA.

UNDER AUTHORITY OF PUBLIC LAW 975, 84TH CONGRESS, APPROVED AUGUST 3, 1956, 4 UNKNOWN AMERICANS WHO LOST THEIR LIVES WHILE SERVING OVERSEAS IN THE ARMED FORCES OF THE UNITED STATES DURING THE KOREAN CONFLICT WERE EXHUMED FROM THE NATIONAL CEMETERY OF THE PACIFIC IN HAWAII. ON MAY 15, 1958, MASTER SERGEANT NED LYLE, U.S. ARMY, HOLDING A CARNATION WREATH STOOD MOMENTARILY SILENT BEFORE THE FOUR IDENTICAL FLAG-DRAPED CASKETS; HE PLACED THE WREATH ON THE END CASKET TO SIGNIFY THE SELECTION OF THE KOREAN WAR UNKNOWN. THE REMAINING UNKNOWN AMERICANS WERE REINTERRED IN THE NATIONAL CEMETERY OF THE PACIFIC.

THE UNKNOWN OF KOREA WAS TRANSPORTED TO THE CRUISER CANBERRA TO JOIN THE UNKNOWNS OF WORLD WAR II.

AT SEA OFF NORFOLK, VIRGINIA, THE UNKNOWNS OF WORLD WAR II AND KOREA WERE TRANSFERRED TO THE DESTROYER BLANDY, WHICH BROUGHT THEM TO THE NATION'S CAPITOL. UPON THEIR ARRIVAL, ON MAY 28, 1958, THE UNKNOWNS WERE TAKEN TO THE ROTUNDA OF THE NATION'S CAPITOL TO REST IN STATE UNTIL MEMORIAL DAY, MAY 30, 1958. THE UNKNOWNS WERE THEN MOVED TO THE MEMORIAL AMPHITHEATER IN ARLINGTON NATIONAL CEMETERY AND THERE, BEFORE DISTINGUISHED GUESTS, THE PRESIDENT AWARDED THE MEDAL OF HONOR TO EACH. AFTER THE SERVICES, THEY WERE BORNE TO THIS PLAZA, AND, FOLLOWING RELIGIOUS RITES, THEY RECEIVED A 21 GUN SALUTE. THE SERVICES WERE CONCLUDED WITH THE FIRING OF THREE VOLLEYS AND THE SOUNDING OF TAPS.

Bottom, far left: the U.S. Treasury Department, considered one of the nation's finest Greek Revival buildings. Top left: the Capitol. Top right: some of the old houses on Lafayette Square which were restored by John F. Kennedy. Left, above and top center: the quiet streets of suburban Washington. Center: one of the attractive embassy buildings on Massachusetts Avenue.

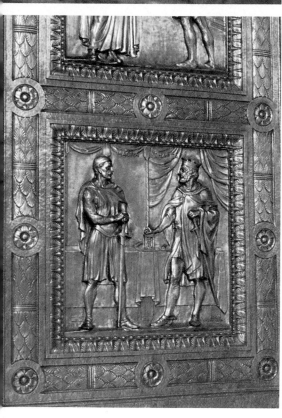

Facing page: (top left) the Capitol; (top right) the Statuary Hall within the Capitol; (bottom left) the Supreme Court and (bottom right) the Washington Monument. This page: (above) a panel from the bronze doors of the Supreme Court (top left); (top right) the Sculpture Garden of the Hirshhorn Museum; (center right) the monument to Spencer Fullerton Baird and (right) the Roman-style National Visitor Center. Overleaf: scenes around the city.

Constructed at the turn of the century, the Library of Congress (these pages) houses one of the largest and finest collections of books in the world. As well as serving its many visitors, the library also provides Congress with valuable research facilities.

The statue of Andrew Jackson (left and top right) stands before the White House. His victory at New Orleans in 1815 raised morale after the British burning of Washington in 1814. Above: the Capitol.

Left: the Smithsonian Instition Building was built in the Norman style in 1855 and is known as "the Castle." Above: the Bureau of Engraving and Printing. Facing page: the Iwo Jima Memorial, which honors the marines killed in battle, depicts five marines and a sailor raising the American flag on Mt. Suribachi, Iwo Jima. Overleaf: (top left) the grand, Classical facade of the U.S. Treasury, (center left) the space-age design of Dulles International Airport, (bottom left) looking east towards the Lincoln Memorial, the Washington Monument and, in the distance, the Capitol, the magnificent dome of which is shown (right), illuminated against a flame-red sky. Inset: the reproduction of the famous Liberty Bell.

55

The Capitol of the United States (top left) was begun in 1793, but was burnt down by the British in 1814. Rebuilding began almost at once and in 1850 alterations added the dome. Today, the West Front is crumbling and repairs are necessary. Above: the Supreme Court. Right: the White House. Inset left: Mount Vernon. Inset right: Marine Corps War Memorial.

On the night of April 14, 1865, President Lincoln was shot in Ford's Theatre (right) and taken to Petersen House (above) before he died next morning. Top left: Watergate, where the most famous scandal of the century began. Top right: the John F. Kennedy Center for the performing arts.

These pages: older than Washington itself, the elegant neighborhood of Georgetown contains many fine Federal-style houses as well as the impressive Georgetown University (below) and the picturesque Chesapeake and Ohio Canal (bottom). Overleaf: the Apollo Lunar Landing Module in the National Air and Space Museum.

CLB 1058
© 1987 Illustrations and text: Colour Library Books Ltd.,
Godalming, Surrey, England.
Text filmsetting by Acesetters Ltd., Richmond, Surrey, England.
Printed and bound in England by Maclehose & Partners Ltd.
1989 edition published by Crescent Books, distributed by Crown Publishers, Inc.
ISBN 0 517 26301 7
h g f e d c b